ISBN 978-0-483-18629-5
PIBN 10587856

THE DEFECTION DETECTED; OR, FAULTS Laid on the RIGHT SIDE.

In Answer to a certain Anonymous PAMPHLET, entitled, *The* DEFECTION Consider'd, &c.

Victrix Causa Deis placuit, sed victa Catoni. Lucan.

LONDON;

Printed by *J. Peters* near *Westminster*. 1718. (Price Six Pence.)

The Defection *Detected, or Faults laid on the Right Side*, &c.

WHatsoever Pretences some Men may make to *Patriotism*, and the *Love of their Country*; whatsoever Disguises they put on to bewilder and deceive the Sight of unheedy Spectators; In a Word, whatsoever Appearances of *Angels of Light* those *Ministers of Darkness* and obscure Practices may assume to themselves; 'tis most incontestably true, that those who look beyond the Surface of Affairs, and have at Heart due enquiries into Things and Occurrences, will distinguish between fallacious Argumentations, and Facts that are supported by right Reasoning. This is the Business of my present Undertaking, how unequal soever I may seem to it; in engaging with an Antagonist that has Power and Authority on his Side, and lies intrench'd under the Ramparts of August Majesty and Parliamentary Bulwarks; and this with all Deference to the Regal Diadem and those Illustrious Personages that stand by the Defence of its just Prerogatives, I intend to pursue with that Closeness and Succinctness, whereby it is necessary to recover injudicious Minds from the most fatal Prepossessions.

To accuse Gentlemen, who are irreproachable for Loyalty, and Conduct, of want of both; to arraign them for Ingratitude and Treachery; to insult them with odious Misrepresentations; are Actions so flagrant, and offensive to good Manners, that (let the Quality of the Person so doing, or so encouraging to be done, be never so great, or conspicuous,) the Injustice of so criminal a Demeanour calls loudly for the Animadversion of such as have any Regard for unsullied Reputations, and unblameable Characters.

When *Crœsus* his Son, that was Tongue-ty'd and Dumb before, saw the uplifted Scymiter ready to make a Sacrifice

crifice of his Father, he burst through all the Ligaments and Impediments of uttering the Sentiments of his Soul, and spoke with an Ardor suitable to the Importance of the Occasion; nor can I, when two of the Fathers of my Country, of high and Patrician Dignity, nay more of Consular Authority, have their Integrity called in Question, their good Names traduced, and their Steadfast Adherence to the Principles of Duty to their Sovereign and Affection to their Fellow Subjects, injuriously treated, be silent and unconcern'd: Especially when the Writer whom I am entering the Lists with, the Author of *The Defection consider'd*, has gone into such unaccountable Lengths of Scandal and Detraction.

A Man of any *Consideration* in the World, before he enter'd upon such a Dirty Work as that of being Scavenger to a Party in Distributing about their Collection of Filth, would, when he was got into the Fit of *Considering*, have turn'd his Thoughts back upon the Transactions of past Years, and have observ'd from the Figures the Lord *Townshend* and Mr. *Walpole* made in them,

them, how much the *Whigs*, owe to their Activity and Zeal, their Courage, and their Conſtancy: He would have given ſome Allowances to the Firſt, for imagining that there was ſome Merit on his Side for concluding the *Barrier Treaty*, without which the *Proteſtant Succeſſion* in the Preſent Illuſtrious Houſe had been precarious; and have pay'd a juſt Deference to the Services of the laſt, in his laſt Unarm'd Endeavour to promote the Publick Good, to advance the Honour of the Britiſh Nation, and to make it appear ſo conſiderable abroad, as to have its due Weight, and in Reality hold the Ballance of *Europe*. In a Word, he would have had an Eye to both of their Paſt Sufferings, and in the Quality of a *VVhig-Writer*, not have left unremark'd on what Account the One was voted by thoſe in a Contrary Intereſt, *an Enemy to his Country*, and the other *ſent to the Tower*: I ſay, he would have much rather have brought in the Government endebted to them on that Score, than have made them Debtors to the Government.

It is not here to be deny'd, but both these Great Men have been amply rewarded, with the highest Posts in the Kingdom, the Confidence of a most indulgent Master, and the Favours of their Prince, yet at the same Time it is altogether as uncontrovertible, that because they stood possess'd of Dignities and Exalted Stations, and had the Countenance of their Soveraign, they were under an Obligation of acting in Complyance with all Measures to be propos'd to them. Far be it from me, any ways to insinuate to what it is not fitting for one in my Sphere to think of, but I hope, it may without Offence be said, that according to Customs in Practice with *Englishmen*, it lies as much in the Breast of a Servant to quit an Employment under the best of Masters, as it does in that of the Masters to discharge, and turn off the Servant: Since to go on and pursue the Drudgery and Fatigue of Business without any Reluctance, even when the former had got a sufficient Competency for his Maintenance without it, might savour of too Covetous a Temper, and make him justly

liable

liable to Censures, and it might carry the Appearance of Hardship in the Latter to demand the Countinuance of such a Man's Labours, that has like the Spider almost spun out his very Bowels in his Service, beyond his Abilities and Strength.

I speak this in Remembrance of Mr. *W———le's* late Escape from the Jaws of Death, by his Recovery from an Illness which at that Time of Day struck those who were most violent for the Court Interest, into the most dreadful Consternation, and, which I defie all that have any Knowledge of that Gentleman's indefatigable Application to the Duties of his Office, not to acknowledge to be the Effect of a Constitution, impair'd and weaken'd by his continued and uninterupted Studies to bring the Administration of Affairs into a right Method at home, and to settle our Negotiations abroad upon a sure and certain Foundation. The Punctual Discharge of the Debts, (as far as in him lay) due upon the Civil Lists, the Appropriation of the respective Funds to them several Uses, the Calculation of what

what was owing by the Nation from Parliamentary Security, the Method of Paying off those Incumbrances with little or no Burthen to the Subjects, the lowering the Interest of Money borrow'd by the Crown to the General Satisfaction of the Lenders, the Tripple Alliance with *France* and *Holland*, the Concessions obtain'd from *Spain*, for the Benefit of Our South Sea-Trade, are such amazing Instances of his Wisdom and Penetration, as must of Course recommend him to the Admiration of the present Age, and the Imitation of that which is to come.

But the Subject Matter of what I am engaged in, from the Pamphlet now under Consideration calls upon me to make good my Assertions in my Title, and to let that Author know, that I am to seek for what he can mean by saying, *he will not detract from the former* Merit of the last Ministry abovenamed, when the Purport of his whole Design, is to expose them for having none; and that I am at a loss for his Branching out his Discourse into Three Divisions, after he has made prophane and Sacred Writ, to ſally together in the Frontiſpiece, unleſs it be to put his Maſters in Mind that he is a Clergyman, and having already obtain'd a Deanery for his *Conduct of the War*, would put them in Mind of a *Conge d' Elire* for his Endeavouring to *break the Peace* under the Specious Pretence of healing Diviſions, and quieting civil Broils and Diſſentions.

To diſplay the Hiſtorian, and Harrangue us with the Conſequences of Inteſtine Diviſions from *Joſephus* his Account of the Downfall of *Jeruſalem*: To bring Teſtimonials from the *Eaſtern VVorld*, that *Conſtantinople*, fell into the Hands of the *Turks*, by the ſame fatal Overſight, and to tell us that the ſame Cauſes have had the ſame Unhappy Effects in the *VVeſtern*: To inform us that we may take it for granted from Biſhop *Burnet's Eccleſiaſtical Hiſtory of the Reformation*, that the Quarrel between the Two Brothers, the Protector and Admiral, brought them both to the Block in King *Edward* the Sixths Reign; and that Queen *Mary was the Popiſh Daughter of* Henry the Eighth: (though

(though it will be difficult for him to prove her, with all his Ecclesiastical Historian's Assistance *born in Incest*,) are Things and Passages he might have spared himself the Trouble of, and which are, it is to be suppos'd, only brought in and introduced, to work upon the Passions of Men liable to Impressions of that Nature, and draw the Reader into a good Opinion of his Bargain, that is etch'd out by such Means into Seven half Sheets.

I shall therefore wave any further Remarks, upon these, and with all necessary Brevity, Account with him in more material Points. The First of which, after his laying it down for an irrefragable Maxim, that *the Purity of Honest* Men, *will never be large*, hits a Box on the Ear, with a vengance on a certain prevailing Party, whose Numbers make them uppermost, is his Concern for the Contentment of *Foreigners* and *Strangers*, which he tacitly implies to be nearer at Heart to him, that the Repose of his own Countrymen; *they'll look on the Divisions with Amazement*, says he; Even ſo be it, let them look their Eyes out; One would think, here was at leaſt a Civil War ſet on Foot, and Hoſtilities enter'd into, between Fellow Subjects, and Brerhren, when the whole Contention here is nothing elſe, on the one Side, but a warm Concern for the Good of the Publick, which none but *Foreigners*, and *Strangers* can be *amaz'd at*, and amounts to no more on the other, than that all Perſons cannot think and act alike. He might, with full as good Reaſon have ſaid, the *Dutch* will *look with Amazement* upon our accountable Security from the Storms and Inundations which they have ſuffer'd by, and out of Pity to *Aliens* and *Strangers*, ſhew ſome Tokens of diſpleaſure, that the ſame Deluges of the devouring Sea, that had made waſte of other Countrys, had not done the ſame by ours.

We are to pleaſe Foreigners------- What Foreigners does he mean? 'Tis to be hoped that we ſhall *pleaſe our Selves*, by a happy Union; by a juſt Obſervation of the Laws already enacted, and by promulging ſuch others as ſhall be

an

an everlasting Fence to the Liberties of Old *England*, and the Preservation of those Rights that have been convey'd down to us, inviolate and undiminish'd by our Ancestors, that procured us the Enjoyment of them. I would not, in this Place, be misconstrued, or judg'd to have the least Retrospect to any Persons of Foreign Extraction now amongst us, who have the same Soveraign with us, and who are under Fealty to the same Head and Governour. These are our Fellow Subjects in one Respect, and want nothing but the *Names* of *Natives* to be our *Friends* and *Brethren*; and these by reciprocal Ties we are under the strictest Obligation to maintain and cultivate mutual Amity with; So that neither the Writer of the *Defection consider'd*, nor my self could have *these* in our Thoughts, at the mention of the Persons before introduced, under the Name of Strangers, though it has been said that some Gentlemen of considerable *Note*, *that* have lately laid down, have not been so very circumspect upon that Topick, but have treated

ted them with more Freedom, than ſhall take upon me to make uſe of.

Had the L——d *T———nd* or Mr. *W———le* advis'd *Royal Viſitations*, had they been for giving up the *Rights of Preſentation to Eccleſiaſtical Benefices*; had they offer'd to give a helping Hand *to a Comprehenſion in Religion*, or made it their Endeavour to introduce all Sects and Perſuaſions to live at Diſcretion within the Incloſures, and feed upon the Paſtures of the Eſtabliſhed Church, well indeed might it have been an Occaſion of Wonder and Surprize. But, for Perſons of Honour to make a Surrender of Offices that cannot be kept without acting counter to their own Principles, and Inclinations; for theſe I ſay to make their Intereſt give Place to their Judgment, and to poſtpone all ſelfiſh and private Views to the Publick, it is ſo far from a Matter of *Amazement*, that it is juſtly one of *Expectation*, and the Reſult of a *Solid* and well grounded *Senſe* of *Duty* and *Allegiance*, rather than of *Pet*, *Whim*, *Humour*, and *Paſſion*.

A

A Skillful Physician in Extraordinary Cases may give into the Use of Extraordinary Remedies, and when the Cure seems desperate, have recourse to *Amputations*, *Causticks*, &c. In like manner may Ministers of State act in Times of Necessity and apparent Danger, when the Pulse of the Disaffected beat high, and one of our Seats of Learning was not free from the Contagion, when Conspiracies were set on Foot to Embroil the Government, and there were no others in Hopes of Tranquility but from going out of the beaten Road of Authority and Power; then it was, and not till then that our Patriots at Helm, (amongst whom the Counsels of the Noble Peer and Gentleman just mentioned were not of the least Weight) thought fit to preserve the Peace by due Care and Circumspections, in Quartering Soldiers upon the University of *Oxford*. But no sooner were the Tumults quash'd, and the Insurrections in *Scotland*, and the North of *England* suppress'd; no sooner had all Appearances of further Commotions ceas'd, and that Illustrious Seminary of Arts and Sciences had a

due

due Senſe of their Submiſſion to their Superiors, by an inoffenſive and unblameable behaviour, but theſe two Miniſters thought it high Time that this Fountain of Knowledge ſhould be ſuffer'd to run clear and undiſturbed, and moſt effectually made uſe of their Intereſt with their gracious Maſter, to cauſe the removal of the unwellcome Gueſts that troubled and diſcolour'd its Chryſtalline Streams.

Nor, are we, as *Natives*, leſs endebted to them for their Love of their Country, than for their incouragement of Learning, if we conſider the ſudden departure and diſcharge of our faithful Allies the *Dutch*. As the unhappy Situation of our Affairs during the late Rebellion, made their coming over hither indiſpenſible, ſo it was likewiſe neceſſary when the Buſineſs they came upon was done and compleated, that they ſhould return to their own Country. To whom their ſudden and expeditious Arrival, and their quick Diſmiſſions of moſt Right to be attributed, I leave to the Judgment of the impartial, ſince if he that managed the Diſpatches of State,

was

was not a Principal in one, and he that was, at the Head of the Treaſury had not a very great Hand in the other, it will be a Work of ſome Difficulty to let us know who had.

Yet theſe and other Services are to be overlook'd. When they were in Place, how were they not careſs'd and adored! Now they are out of Employment, how not derided and vilified! As, if Reaſon, Eloquence and Merit, were annexed to an Office, and thoſe Excellencies of Precaution and Management that made them the Objects of the *Whigs* Admiration and Eſteem before, had no longer Duration than their abode in Courts: As if to be diſſatisfied with ſome Men's Proceedings, was to Act in Diſobligation of all the whole Party, and to refuſe an implicit Aſſent to ſome of their Fellow-Servants Schemes, was to Act in Contempt of their Maſter's.

Such falſe Reaſoning as this may in all Probability, have an Influence upon Men, that ſwallow Party Writings greedily, and take every Thing for granted, that's ſpoken on their own ſide; but Men diveſted of Prejudice, of calm and ſedate Apprehenſions will ſoon make a Diſcovery of the Fallacy, and rightly diſtinguiſh between Paſſion and Deliberation, Diſguſt and Prudence. Were I to aſk the Opinion of the latter concerning Mr. *W——le*'s Conduct in his late Reſignation of his Commiſſion, whether it was out of *Pet* or *Policy*, I am well nigh perſwaded he would fix the Cauſe upon the latter, and conclude with *Matchiarel*, that for a Miniſter of State to keep the Steerage at Helm, while " his Friends and Re-" lations are in Diſgrace, is to run the " Riſque of the ſame Fate himſelf.

Therefore the Libeller muſt give me leave to refer him to the Practices of States-men in former Reigns, wherein, almoſt every one, he will meet with frequent Precedents of this Nature; and find that the greateſt Favourites have ever behaved in the ſame manner as Mr. *W——le*, howſoever attach'd in their Devoirs to their Sovereign, or Zeal for the Service of the Publick; To lead him no farther back than the late Queen's time, he may there ſee, by the

the Demeanour of the *Whig* Courtiers at the displacing of the Duke of *M——ough* and the Treasurer, the Earl of *Godolphin*, that several Lords whose Services were equally as necessary to Queen *Anne*, as Mr. W—-*le*'s to his present Majesty, sought their Quietus at a Juncture, when she was under the utmost Embarrassment, as to the Affairs of Her Allies, and the Peace then in Agitation. It was thought no Crime in them to go over to the Country Party, who were averse to the Measures set on Foot by the Court; and can it with Justice be imputed to this Gentleman and his Honourable Associates as a Fault, that he trades in the steps, they themselves have mark'd out for him? This very Cavil is enough to make appear that this mighty Pretender to *Secret's* know's not so much of what has been, or is upon the Carpet, as he would assume to himself the Reputation; and makes it to be much suspected, whether any great Man be at the Bottom of his Correspondence or Intelligence: Because it is highly absurd to instance in Particulars, which, there is not one of all the Nobility, but must assuredly know, and plead in Justification the Procedure that is here censur'd.

Nor is the Person that takes upon him the Espousal of a Quarrel, which has no need of such a Defender, less unhappy in his *Definitions*, than the other Branches of his positive and wise Declamations, as evidently appears from his Characters of the two contending Parties. "The *Whig Party*, *says he*, by "their Principles are for a limited Mo-"narchy, so the House of *Hanover*: for "the *Church*, and *Regal Supremacy*, all "by Law, established; for *tolerating* the "*Protestant Dissenters* at home, and "freeing them from those Hardships, "they were lately put under for their "Zeal to the *Protestant Religion*, and "the *Protestant Succession*; and for "treating those abroad as becomes the "Head of the Common Protestant In-"terest. For encouraging *Trade*, *Ma-*"*nufactures*, *Industry*, and every thing "that tends to the publick Good?

"The other Party (*viz.*) that of the "Tories, bring by their Principles for "*absolute Power* in the *Popish Line*, are

"of

" of course, Enemies to *Liberty*, *Property*,
" and the *Protestant Religion*; are for
" a strict Union with the most bigot-
" ted *Papists*; for setting up a Papal
" Indepency in their own Clergy; for
" confounding the Reformed abroad,
" as well as at home, and for discou-
" raging by their persecuting, and o-
" ther pernicious Maxims, all *Trade*,
" *Manufacture*, *Industry*, and every
" Thing that's for the Publick Good?

Now, in Respect to the first Definition (that of a Whig) is it possible for any one to be for the *Church*, who has the least Eye towards breaking in upon the Act of Uniformity, which he must have, that has any Thoughts of bringing about a *Comprehension*? Or how can they be for asserting the *Regal Supremacy*, whose Principles teach them to *bind their Kings in Chains, and their Nobles in Fetters of Iron?* As for my Antagonist's joining *Religion* and *Trade* together; it evidently shews he's of that Sect, that makes a *Trade* of *Religion*; and while he screens himself under the Protection of the sacred Name of the *Church*: (What *Church* he is no way particular in) he gives us tacitly to underſtand, that he's a downright *Leveller*, and by repealing the Schiſm Act is the only Security, next to God and the King of the *Eſtabliſh'd Faith*, would put Proteſtants of all Degrees and Opinions, upon the ſame Bottom. And much good may it do him, ſay I, to boaſt himſelf one of a Party; who, by theſe means, would defeat the Hopes we have, of a long Race of Kings from the *Proteſtant Succeſſion*, rather than encourage them; Since ſuch a Motley Medley of *Religion*, equal to each other in Power and Authority, would ſet aſide all Succeſſions whatſoever, except thoſe of Anarchy and Confuſion, which would be unlimited as well as perpetual. As for my Part, howſoever the Character is made black and odious by ſcandalous Miſrepreſentations; may, I ever fall under the Cenſure of joining with the Tories, who inſtead of being for *abſolute Power* in the *Popiſh Line*, are not for ſuch a *Power* in any; and tho' they do not engroſs all the Merit of the *Revolution*, that preſerved our *Liberty*, *Property*, and the

Pro-

Protestant-Religion, have a *Right* to value themselves upon their being the Projectors of the Settlement of the Succession of the Crown in the House of *Hanover*; and of strengthening and securing that Settlement, by proposing and drawing up most or all of the subsequent Acts of Parliament, that were made in Confirmation of it. So that if the Lord *T---nd*, and Mr *W---le* are gone over to the last of these Parties, they are far ftom uniting themselves, with those that are in a strict *Alliance with the most bigotted Papists*, for setting up a Papal Independency, for confounding the Reformed, abroad and at home, and for discouraging *Trade*, *Manufacture*, *Industry*, &c. Because it is as clear as the Sun at Noon Day: They hold their *Bishops* to be subordinate to the King, who is justly stiled the *Defender of the Faith*, and has the Nomination to all the vacant Sees: Neither are they so senseless, who malicious soever they are represented to be, as to be for the *Confusion* of the *Reformed* in general; since such an Extensive, ill-natur'd Design would endamage

damage themſelves as well as others, and put them into the Condition of the envious Wretch in the Fable, who was for putting out of his own Eyes, that his Enemy might loſe his. The laſt Charge upon the *Tories* in the foregoing Character, is as irrational and undeſerved, as the reſt, as will appear from the greateſt and moſt profitable *Branch* of our Trade, that of our Commerce in the *South Seas*, which owes it's Riſe and Eſtabliſhment to the *Party* thus ſtigmatiz'd and abus'd, and had not now been in being; but for a certain Lord that will never have ſome People's Pardon, for an Invention ſo uſeful to Traffick, and the Support of Publick Credit.

But all the *Tories*, even *Hanover Tories* amongſt the reſt, are to be ſet forth with Marks of Infamy and Shame, that theſe worthy Patriots and their Followers, who have done them the Honour of thinking them not in the wrong, by voting with them, may be blacken'd and traduced amongſt the Number. They are changed with *Lying*, *Perjury*, *Embroiling* the *Nation* in a Civil a Civil War, contrary to the express Sentiments of the King and Parliament themselves, who laid the whole blame of the late Rebellion on the *Papists*; and some few misled Malecontents from the Dregs of the Populace, that this Noble Peer and his Brother in Law, might come in for their Share of those odious Imputations; even while, (as it has been already observed) the Suppression of those very Commotions was effected by their Diligence, and provident Dispositions. Nay, what is more surprizing, and has a much juster Title to call upon the Amazement of all Mankind (*Foreigners* as well as *Natives*) than the Quarrel of Great Men among themselves: Our *Pamphleteer* has the Hardiness to take even greater *Liberties*, and turns the Artillery of Count *Gyllenborgh*'s Letters, that were Intercepted and Publish'd, while they were at the Head of Affairs against themselves. Could any thing savour of greater Insolence and Injustice, than the offering this Violence to common Honesty and good Manners? Than the committing of this Rape upon Sense

 and

and all human Probability? For he muſt have a very mean and low Opinion of their *fine* and *florid Parts*, that could imagine them to be ſo faint and depraved on a ſudden, as not to withold them from expoſing their own Guilt, by ſuffering thoſe Papers, wherein Mention was made of their Names to their Diſadvantage, to ſee the Light. Nothing is more certain, than that it was in their Power to have conceal'd them; and that, if there had been any Criminal Correſpondence between Mr. *W------le* and that *Swediſh* Miniſter, it would not have been left in the Breaſt of any Perſon whatſoever, to have made a Diſcovery of it. The Warrant for the Seizure of the Count and his Papers, came through the Hands of my Lord *T------nd*, who gave it into Major General *Wade*'s Hands to execute. The Major General, in Purſuance of his Orders, brought the Papers to this Noble Peer, who had them in his Poſſeſſion long enough, before they were examin'd by his Majeſty and the Council, to have an Opportunity, if any Thing Criminal therein related to himſelf

ſelf or Mr. W-----*le*, of ſcreening what he judg'd proper to be ſecret, or made away with, and would not have now been envied for that Readineſs of Thought, that makes him dreaded by his Enemies, and belov'd by his Friends, had he not done it. But Innocence is fearleſs and unſuſpicious: They both of them knew their Fidelity to their Maſter, and had ſo great and intire a Belief in their Maſters juſt Eſteem, for their unſhaken Steadineſs in his Service, that no Artifices whatſoever could gain Ground upon him to their Prejudice; eſpecially, ſuch *obſcure* and dark *Paſſages*, as it could not enter into the Breaſt of their moſt inveterate Enemies, to turn into any thing like a Traiterous Correſpondence: They therefore were as forward in their Advice for the Publication of the Counts Letters, as any Noble Perſons at the Council Board, which Act of theirs muſt abſolve them from all Manner of Guilt, or condemn that Aſſaſſin of good Names and Characters, that endeavours to give a private Stab to their Reputations by

Innu-

Innuendos, for ſpeaking well of their Abilities in Political Concerns.

Nor is their Intimacy with a General in Diſgrace to be imputed to them as a Crime, ſince the Politeneſs of that General, who is *tam Marte quam Mercurio*, is engaging enough to recommend him to the Converſation of thoſe, who may think themſelves in a contrary Intereſt. The Reſpects he is entituled to from his conſtant Attachment to the Succeſſion of the Family now upon the Throne; the Deference he ever pay'd to a certain Prince in *Flanders*, when his high Deſerts and Quality were overlook'd and under-rated by another great Officer in the Army, the Conduct and Favour his Merits obtain'd for him for ſome time with his Majeſty and his Royal Predeceſſor; his valorous Exploits during the whole Courſe of the laſt War, and the Laurels he reap'd by putting a glorious End to the late Rebellion in *Scotland*, were Inducements enough to plead in Excuſe for Men of Merit themſelves to be Ambitious of his Company: So, that if the Patriots above-named had a juſt and becoming

Regard

Regard for his Graces noble Atchievements, and most excellent Qualities; though, he whom they pay'd their Respects to, was envied and out of Place, they acted with much more Truth and Sincerity, than our CONSIDERER, who not content to see that General dispoiled of his Posts and Preferments, gives the Honour and Reputation of *crushing* a most dangerous Rebellion ito another, who knows how to make use of, and turn to a very good Account other Men's Victories.

The same *Detractor* of an Author, might also have spared the Mention of *Foreign Divorces*, *New Marriages*, and his other *idle Tales*, or if he could not keep a Secret, ought to have laid it at the Right Party's Door; Since Mr. W----*le* is known to have the greatest Aversion to such silly Stories, that take their Rise only from the Imagination; and are mere *Entia Rationis*. But he is so given to fasten his Scandal upon wrong Persons, that, as he before ascrib'd the Honour due to a certain Duke, otherwise than it ought, and gave it away to a Lord, who had no

man-

manner of Claim to it: So now he goes on with the ſame Act of Injuſtice, in impoſing upon his Readers, by Fathering Brats of his own Invention upon another Perſon. But this Inſinuation is carryed on and conducted with ſo aukward and ill-favour'd a Grace, that any one poſſeſs'd of little *Wiſdom*, *Sagacity*, or *Penetration*, may ſee through the Deſign which lies open and diſcoverable, and ſhews, that thoſe who, in Reality, *diſtreſs the King's Affairs*, would lay the blame of their own Actions upon thoſe that do not.

Would it anſwer the Time to be ſpent on ſuch an un-edifying Subject, I could here point out the Blunder's and Inconſiſtencies, this SELF CONTRADICTER is guilty of: I could run over the ſeveral Eſcapes, he makes from his own Memory, and ſhew that he affirms in one Place, what he denies in another. I could bring him in ranging one Sentence in Battle-array againſt another, and make him ſo well skill'd in the Art of Forgetfulneſs, as to ſay in one Page, that *it is impoſſible for them to ſucceed*, and in Six or Seven

Pages

Pages farther ask the Queſtion, whether they *will not ſucceed in their Attempts?* In this, to inſinuate, that the Perſons who are under *his Conſideration,* or rather cenſure, *have Judgments none of the ſoundeſt, and Reputations none of the beſt,* and in that, to change his Note, and declare them *the moſt able, nay, the moſt honeſt States Men this Nation was ever bleſs'd with.* To make Mr. *W------le* get *incredible Sums* in one Paragraph, to offer 90000 *l. for a ſingle Purchaſe* in another, and then to ſtrip him quite naked again, and reduce him to his former neceſſitous Circumſtances in a Third, by making his *Fortune ſtill deſperate:* In a Word, to cry up and highly applaud the Conduct of the *Perſon now at the Head of the Treaſury,* here; and there, to ſay, that the *Credit of the* Whigs *is ſunk very low in Town and Country,* are Inſtances enough to convince any one that is not deaf to Conviction, that he is much more inconſiſtent with himſelf, than thoſe whom he endeavours to repreſent in the moſt odious Colours, halloos his Canine Yelping Accuſations at, and with

with Indignities, for being Deserters of their former Principles.

Crimine ab uno ----- Disce omnes.

From the Passages just taken notice of, it will not be difficult to make an Estimate of the rest of the Incoherencies, which this *Jumble* of Flattery and Scandal abounds with. I shall therefore proceed from his causeless Reflections upon Sir *Ed. N----thy*, (who cannot be said to have been neglectful of the Duties of his Post, either as to Impeachments or Tryals) to the Charge brought in against Mr. *W----le*, as the only Person that occasion'd the Earl of *Oxfords* lying so long in Prison, before he was brought to Justice, and occasion'd his Acquitment, when he was. The Transactions at the Tryal of that Noble Peer, are so fresh in every one's Memory, that he must have a Forehead, of something more substantial than Brass, who can give himself an Air of Assurance like this; since the Number of the Gentlemen that compos'd the Secret Committee has been

ascer-

ascertain'd in the Votes of the House of Commons; and it is very well known, that though Mr. *W----b* was in the Chair for some time, he had no such Influence and Authority over the rest of the Members as to prevent any Motion for bringing that Lord to his Trial, or when brought, to make their Proceedings of no Effect against him. The Lords were his *Judges*, and the Commons his *Accusers*, and if the *first* acquitted him, because the *last* would not give into the Methods of Trial, which they conceiv'd contrary to the Usage of Parliaments, where is there the least Ground of Calumny against the Gentleman to whose Share the whole Odium of that noble Earl's being declared innocent most ungenerously falls. The Articles against him were ready prepared; his Answer was given into the House of Lords, and the Common's *Replication* was drawn up and deliver'd; so that nothing was wanting in Mr. *W----le*, who gave his Consent, and had a Hand in the Specification of every Treason and High Crime he was accused of, to do justice to the Nation in whose name the Prosecution was brought, by a speedy dy and expeditions Trial. But this was a Scandal of Weight and Importance, and highly necessary to be hammer'd out of the Forge of Infamy and Detraction, as being Popular and Capable of Spiriting up the People against him.

The Comparison between him and the late Treasurer is likewise very artfully made to blacken and asperse him, but it may perhaps fall Short of its Design of it, even tho' the Story of the Yatch, the 250000 *l*, and the House at *Chelsea* were true. For there are some Acts of Parliament owing to that Earl, amongst which that of settling and further securing the Protestant Succession is not to be forgotten, that demonstrates him to be of a publick Spirit, and have at Heart the Love of his Country, which the little Wealth he acquir'd by a Four Years Administration of the Affairs of the Treasury, during which he will find it difficult to ptove that more Money was raised, and more Debts incurred than in the Seven Preceding. Nor shall I take this Author's Word, or agree with him in calling that a persecuting Bill, which is an Act

to

to prevent Schiſm, or ſet leſs Value upon a Gentleman who will not give into the Repeal of a Statute, that is the chief Bulwark to keep of the Enemies of the Church Eſtabliſh'd, than upon a *B*—— whom a Committe of Convocation has declared to give up her Rights and thoſe of his own ſacred Order, to be held in common by Men of all Religions and Perſwaſions. Neither ſhall I, tho' Mr. *W*——*le* may not be able to refute Mr. *B*——*ks* pretended Affidavit, which is drawn up without Form or Name to it, and is very much to be ſuſpected on both thoſe Accounts, believe that he is the only Perſon that had made Advantages of the Diſpoſal of Places for himſelf; ſince I have ſeveral Examples of the ſame Nature now upon Recollection, wherein I could particularize Perſons and Things, and could inſtance in both Sexes now living. Why then ſhould that Practice be brought in as Criminal in Him that is allowable in others. *Dat Veniam Corvis vexat censura Columbas.* Some Peoples Quality places them above Animadverſions and Enquiries, tho' if I remember rightly, Mr. *W*——*le*, tho' repreſented *to be*

 none

none of the most modest in asking, is not the Man, who had it in reply from a certain Prince to a certain Question, *that such a venerable Prelate had been sitting with Him two whole Hours, and during all that long, long time, neither ask'd one Grant or Favour for himself or his Friend.* A Flea in the Ear that might have made somebody less importunate than he has been for some time since.

As for what Mr. *W——le* did in the House of Commons, in Relation to the setting up Dr. *Snape*, whom our *inconsiderable* CONSIDERER calls a *Prevaricating Wretch*, to Preach before that Honourable Assembly on the 39th of *January* last, and his seconding the Motion there made for Thanks for his Excellent Sermon, *The Political State of Great Britain*, for the said Month has set that Affair in a true Light, and in that worthy Members own Words; wherein he says, "that he had known "that Excellent Person long; that he "had trusted him with the Education "of his Two Sons, as had the Lord "*T——nd* with one of his; which "Trust he discharged with the utmost

"Fi-

" Fidelity, *&c.* To this may be added a much greater Teſtimony of his Work, the Choice which a whole Univerſity, that of *Cambridge* made of him to repreſent that Learned Body, at the Celebration of the *Jubilee* at *Franckfort* on the *Oder*: And to give ſtill a greater Weight to the Bulk of his Reputation, the Honour that was done him by the late Princeſs *Sophia*, the King's Royal Mother, who was pleas'd to appoint him to Preach before her in Engliſh, as a Mark of the Higheſt Diſtinction, which may moſt aſſuredly put his Merits upon the Ballance with thoſe of Dr. *John Hoadly*, who is Pitch'd upon by the Houſe of Commons, to do the ſame Office on the ſaid Anniverſary this year, if not with the Superior Deſerts of the B. of *B*: who for his High Station in the Church, if for no other Cauſe, muſt have the Preference.

This brings me of Courſe, to our Pamphleteers baſe Reflections on Mr. *W——le*'s Conduct, (who is ſtyled a *bold daring Fellow*, in Page 39, and made to *act a mean cowardly Part*, by way of Antitheſis in Page 43) and his Noble Brother in Laws Conduct, in

Re-

Relation to their opposing the taking off two of the State Holy Days: The Anniversaries of the Martyrdom of King *Ch.* I. and the Restoration of his Son *Charles* II. to the Throne of his Ancestors, which like all the rest of his Arguments and Accusations, only serve to discover his own Weakness and Guilt; and to make the *Tories* appriz'd of Designs in Agitation, that common Prudence would have kept secret till ripe for Execution: *O tell it not in Gath, nor publish it in Askalon*; that a Day set apart for humbling our selves before God, for the inhuman and barbarous Murther of the best of Princes by the worst of Subjects, should ever be attempted to be unobserv'd or expunged out of our Liturgy or Calendar, *lest the Daughters of the Philistines rejoice, and the uncircumcised triumph.* Let it remain hidden to the Eyes of the World, that ever a Set of unthankful Men had it in their Thoughts, to shew their Ingratitude to Heaven, for the greatest of Mercies that could be receiv'd, by the Abolition of a Festival, that has not only the sanction of Parliament to make it perpetual; but the Blessings of the most high God for its solemnization; and this during the

Reign

Reign of a Prince, that owes his Crown and Dignity to his being a Branch of the Royal Family so miraculously Restored. Could any thing more excite our Veneration and esteem for these two illustrious Patriots, than their *coming out from among* a Party (if any such there be) who do not blush to own such abominable Purposes? could it have been in the Power of their heartiest Advocate to have utter'd any thing more in favour of what is call'd their *Defection*, than their refusal to give into Measures so Destructive of their Duty, to God and their King, and so abhorrent of all Compassion and Gratitude: The *Preservation of the Peace* on those days, is a poor, very poor Pretence for their *Non-observance*, and it is easie to see something more than the suppression of Tumults (which might have put him in mind of his Mug-house Riotters) and the setting aside the wearing of a few harmless Oaken Boughs aim'd at by this Author. So that if it was thought high time by some Gentlemen to cease going hand in hnad with others in Schemes quite contrary to the Principles they had imbibed from their Infancy: If their innate Love of their Country and

and the antient Constitution of th
Kingdom, which they had suck'd in wit
their first Breath made them admit o
no variations from what their Father
had taught them: If their Zeal for th
Rights of the Church in the Doctrine
of which they had been happily brough
up, and the Privileges and Immunitie
of the Universities whereof they ha
been Members and Shining Ornaments
If Acts of Mercy when the Sword o
Justice was drawn against Unfortunate
repenting Gentlemen under Sentence o
Death, which even his Majesty himse
out of his Royal Clemency gave int
and which this audacious Writer, i
necessity o

assenting to.

To Conclude, if keeping strictly to th
Letter of some Acts of Parliament made i
Defence of the State, and opposing the R
peal of others now in Force, for the S
curity of the Church, be *of any Praise*
good Report, the Lord *T——nd* and Mr. *W—*
with their Illustrious Associates, are mo
to be celebrated in the History of the
Times, for their Firmness and Courag
their *Self-denyal* and *Zeal*, for their Ki
and Country's Happiness and Tranquilit
than those that make a Merit of calli
their *Resignation* a *Defection*, and their *Reti*
ment from Courts, a Duty and Allegiance

FINIS.

Lightning Source UK Ltd.
Milton Keynes UK
UKHW011149051118
331792UK00005B/276/P